I0511301

Photographing Animals

Book 5
in
Quick Tips by a Pro
Photographer
Series

by Julia Harwood

Table of Contents

1. Special Thanks

I would like to make a special mention of a few people who without their support this series would not be possible. Firstly to my Proof Reader, Cathy Longley, no matter how sick you were you still managed to get these done, thank you so much. The to all my supporters on Pozible but most especially Angela Chan, as without her financial backing this project would not have been possible and finally to my wonderful husband Colin, who put up with me spending so many hours on the computer. I hope these help you on your photographic journey.

You can also follow me on my

website at Photography by Julia K Harwood
http://www.juliaharwood.com/

For all your gift needs
http://www.redbubble.com/people/juliakharwood/portfolio

To follow me on G+
http://plus.google.com/+JuliaHarwood

To follow on FB
http://m.facebook.com/Photography.by.Julia.K.Harwood

To view a gallery of my images

http://photographybyjuliakharwood.shootproof.com/juliaharwood

2. Introduction

Just like photographing people, we need to engage with animals to take good close up images of them or if you want action shots you can be further away.

My book on Portraits also has lots of tips that will help with animals as well. They are just furry people aren't they?
You can get it here
http://www.amazon.com/dp/B00T XS8FQG as an ebook or here https://www.createspace.com/5483 763
as a paperback

One of the main considerations I want you to have when photographing animals is not to stress them and with wild animals, be careful not to get too close to nests or dens, if you do the mother may attack or else abandon the babies, we don't want either to happen.

It is important to learn animal behavior so you know when they feel threatened or scared.

I will cover dogs, cats and horses in this e-book, but the Internet is a great recourse for finding out for other animals, also the zoo will often have keepers that are more than happy to talk to you if you explain that you want to know so that you don't cause them any stress.

It is always a good idea to get the pets owner, a zoo keeper or a safari leader to work with you, as they will know the animals routines and what commands they are used to.

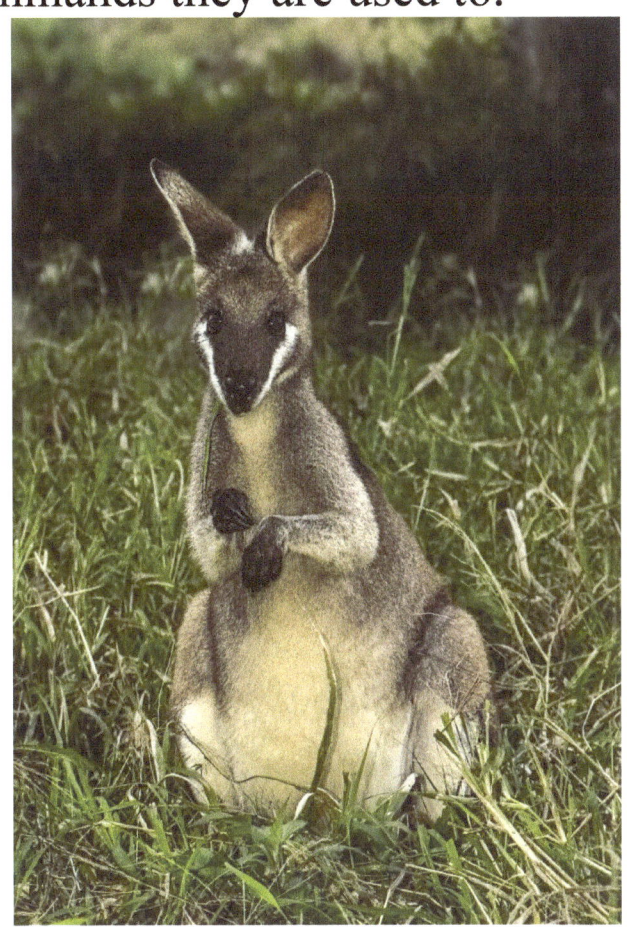

3. Domestic Animals

For domestic animals, these are some of the questions you can ask the owner or you could even email them a questionnaire for them to fill out.

To get you started, ask ...
What toys do they like?
What tricks does he or she do?
Are there any parks or areas that he/she visits regularly?
How do they behave Off leash?
How does your animal react to strangers and other dogs/animals?
Do they know any commands?
Do they have any quirky things or tricks they do?
What are their favorite toys?
Are they food motivated or attention motivated?

How do you get their attention?
Where do they spend most of their time?
What's their favorite spot to be patted or scratched?

Getting early to a shoot and allowing time to just play with the animal and let it get comfortable with you is vital.

We don't want to stress the animal as then we will also end up stressed. Take a few treats or ask the owner to supply some.

If you bring treats check whether the dog has any allergies before using them.

Also carry a few toys with you, animals are notoriously curious so they will be more willing to play if it is a new toy they want to have.

Start with something they are comfortable doing.

Petting the animal and letting them smell you is always a good start.
Be patient with the animal.

Get down to animals level.

To get animals attention and looking at camera you can use food or a toy, even treats lose value over time so start off with just normal animal biscuits and save their favorite treat for getting their attention when everything else fails.

Dogs and cats can be trained by having a small clicker or squeaker that you click or squeak, then give them the treat, they quickly make the association and then click it when you are ready to take shot and they will look at you in expectation.

Give lots of praise as well as treats

If something is distracting the animal, place yourself between animal and distraction

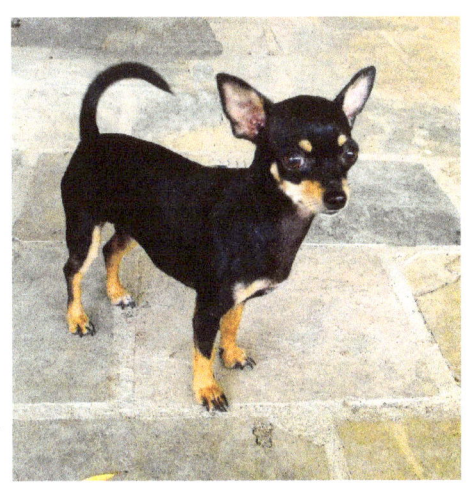

4. Gear to Use

It is important to have the right gear with you and to know what situations to use it in. Better to be prepared and have extra gear in the car than not having the things you need.

Here is a quick checklist, you can add your own to this as well.

Camera
Flash with movable head to bounce is indoors or a lite scoop if outside. Soft box, you can put any light in these.

A lens with as low an f-stop as possible, preferably f1.4 to f2.8 and that also has quick focus and image stabilization.

Lenses with a focal length 85mm for full body and head shot, 35mm more wide angle to show setting, also use for looking down from above at dog, 70-200mm f2.8 action lens is good as it gives you the most options in one lens.

Use the fastest memory card that you can afford, this will allow more burst shots at one time.

Carry a spare battery and spare cards.

Reflector.

A Lens hood, as it protects the lens and keeps dog nose off lens.
If shooting wild animals then a tripod to stabilize the long zoom will help.

Remember to turn Image stabilization (IS) off when using the tripod and turn it back on when you are not.

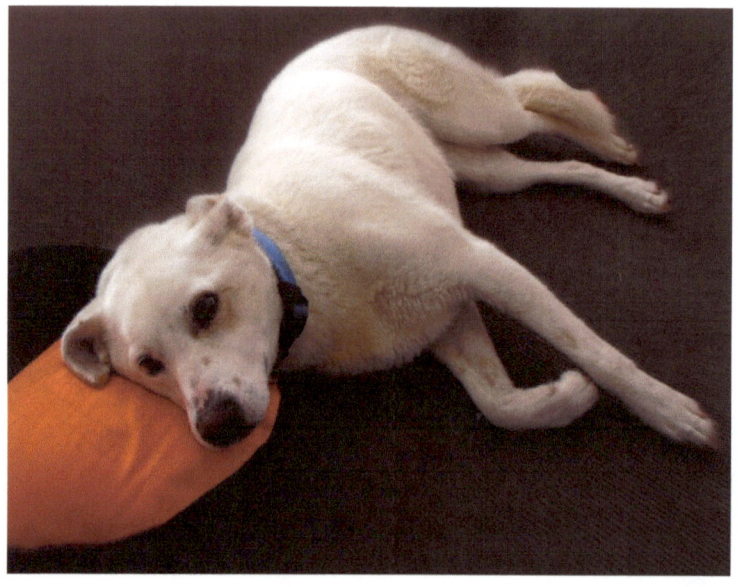

5. Settings

Shutter Speed
It is a good idea to photograph animals at faster shutter speeds, whether your subject is indoors or outdoors.

When animals move, they move fast so try to keep your shutter speed high.

You can do this with the sport's mode on your camera or DSLR, or by setting Shutter Priority or if you are comfortable with your camera's manual settings, choose a shutter speed of 1/500 or higher.

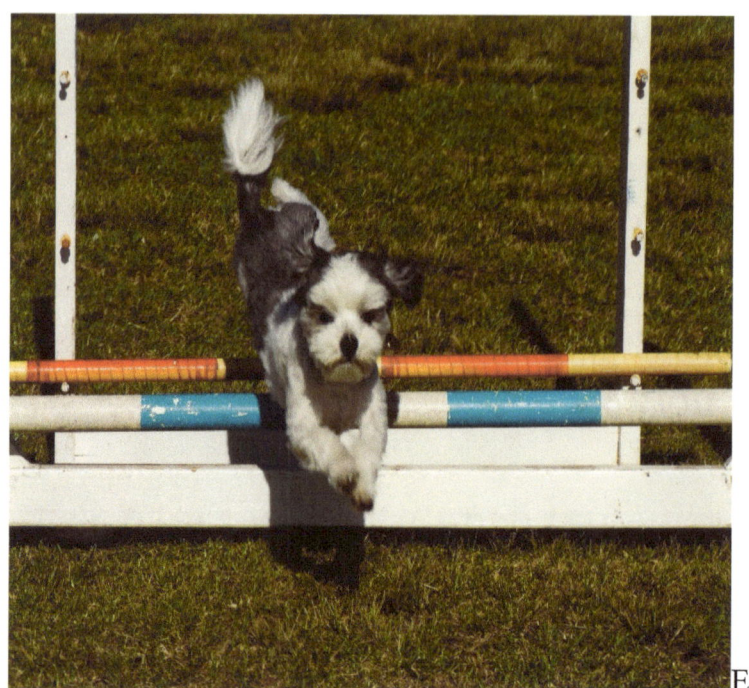

E

Exposure

If going from light to shade use AP or A priority.

If this isn't an issue, use S shutter priority to freeze action.

If the animal is a pet and is calmer and your goal is to capture a portrait-style image, you can use the portrait mode on your camera just as you would when photographing a person.

In manual or semi-manual modes, this means shooting with a large aperture (smaller f-number), which will blur out any unwanted distractions in the background by giving you a shallow depth of field.

Try f 5.6 to f2.8 and make sure focus is on the eyes.

If you want a little more context, use a smaller aperture (larger f-number) f 8-f22 and therefore larger depth of field.

Don't be afraid to turn your ISO up a little bit if you need to.

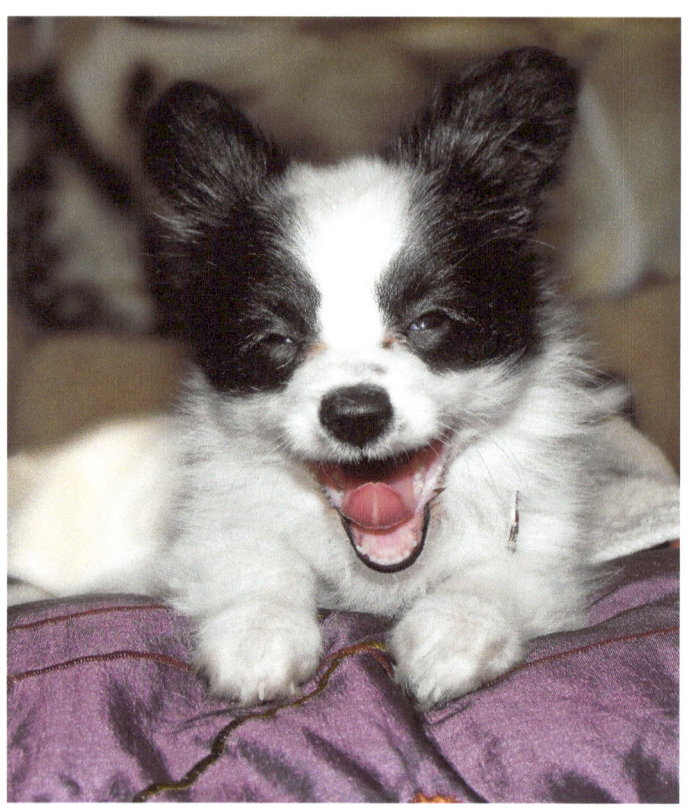

With animals, keep your camera set on burst mode and use continuous servo auto focus. Al, As or C depending on your camera.

This enables you to focus on the animal's eye and it will track that spot as the animal moves.

You may need more precise focusing than you are used to, (especially when shooting at larger apertures), so you should try to make friends with your camera's single-point AF setting.

That's the setting that lets you move the focus point around in the viewfinder using the joystick or control on the back of your camera.

Using a single-point AF will allow you to place that focus point right where you want it over the eye of the animal regardless of the other composition decisions you may decide to make.

You can also focus on the animal and then recompose, the disadvantage of this though, is if the animal moves between the time you set the focus and then recompose, you will miss the correct focus.

Often when photographing animals we want a large zoom lens to get close enough to them.

Remember you will need a shutter speed that is the inverse of the focal length, so I'd your focal length is 500mm you will need a minimum of 1/500 as the shutter speed to hand hold the camera.

Alternatively you can use a tripod, but make sure the shutter speed is still high enough to freeze the movement if that is what you want to do.

When using a large focal length we need to remember that the depth of field becomes narrower, so a setting of f5 at 50mm is more like the depth of field of f2.8 at 500mm even though the camera is still set to f5.

So we need a fast shutter speed to freeze action and a reasonable depth of field, at least f8 if zoomed in, which will often leave you with only one option to correct the exposure and that is to raise the ISO.

So if you want to work with animals, make sure you have a camera that handles high ISO well and also have a good post processing
 program to help remove excess noise in post processing. I use Photoshop and Lightroom and a separate plugin called Topaz

Denoise to ensure I get the best possible result.

Another way to focus with fast moving animals is to set a focus trap.

To do this we focus on a spot where we think the animal will pass through, then when the animal gets here we press the shutter and hold it down to get multiple exposures and have the best chance of getting the money shot.

The next thing is to look at camera angle, we really want to be down at the animals level or lower as this gives a much more interesting perspective than from the standing position.

Sometimes it looks really good if you use a wide angle which will distort the animals features, but otherwise you are best using at a 35-50mm or larger focal length.

To retain detail in face, rather than the whole dog, use a narrow depth of field (f2.8 to f5.6)

If you need more light then use a reflector, a soft box or a fill flash with tissue over it to diffuse it or a lite scoop.

Most animals don't like direct flash as it hurts their eyes and diminishes their ability to see for a short time.

If the image is back lit and you don't want to create a silhouette then use some fill flash.

Most cameras will automatically use fill flash when you set them to aperture priority and turn on the camera's flash.

It is always better to use an off camera flash if you can and preferably with a diffuser or you can bounce the flash off the ceiling if indoors or you can bounce it into a light scoop.

Check that the flash is not going to startle or frighten the animal first.

Often using a reflector to add light is the better option or you can add a red gel or filter to your flash so that it is softer on the animal's eyes.

Fill flash is flash that is less than full power. Most cameras allow you to adjust the strength of the flash in the menu.

To create fill light in a back lit image, position the flash or reflectors as close to subject as possible, the closer the flash or reflectors are the softer the light.

Position it as close to the camera in angle, while being out of shot so you get catch lights in both eyes.

You can use flash during the golden hour to expose the shot to retain color in sky and use the flash to light the animal.

Always check with the animals owner or handler before using flash.

When shooting into the light we often get Lens flare, this can look very artistic if we can control it.

Hold your hand up between the sun and your lens till you get what you are after, watch that your hand doesn't show in the image.

To create lens flare
Position bright light, sun just off camera or in the shot but make sure lens flare is not on face as this detracts from the image.

Indoor light can be good for domestic animals, so if there is a large full length window, place yourself between the dog and the window.

If not look for shaded areas where there is even, soft light.

Light up the eyes as much as possible.

Avoid mixing indoor and outdoor light.

So if you are shooting indoors with window light then turn off indoor lights.

If this does not give you enough light, then move outdoors or close curtains and just use indoor light.

Pay attention to the background. Look for different light sources, for example if are using natural light, turn off overhead lights.

While checking the background look for any distractions and move them if possible, if not, then angle them out or use a narrow aperture, low f stop to blur them out.

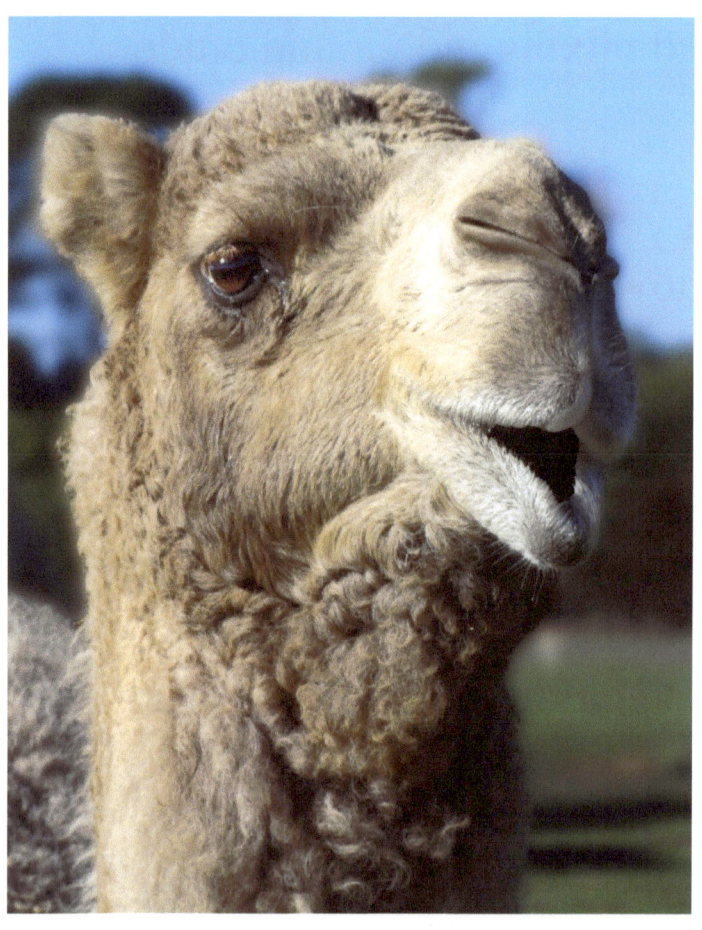

6. Composition

The first thing we look for in any image with eyes in it is that the eyes are in focus and if possible have a catch-light in them.

This enhances our feeling of interacting with the animal which means we are also engaging with the image.

The next thing we need to look at is the background. Will it enhance the shot and give us a sense of place or is it too busy or does it have unwanted objects in it?

If we want to include the objects in the shot, we can use a wide depth of field and a large f stop or if we just want the focus on the animal and to eliminate the background distractions, then we need a narrow depth of field or a small f stop.

Check there are no objects sticking out of the animal's head, and look for bright objects that might cause distractions.

Our eyes are automatically drawn to bright areas. Move elements or yourself to recompose without the distraction.

To do this, see if by moving a little you can angle out unwanted areas in the background, you can also shoot low but facing up, so that the sky is in the background or shoot from above looking down, so you just have the ground as the background.

While looking at camera angle it is best to get down to the animals level, so you are at the same level as their eyes, but remember, safety first, don't put yourself in harms way.

When composing the shot, we want to leave room for the animal to move into, so depending on which direction they are facing as to where you need to leave some space.

In the following picture the tiger is facing to the right, so there is more space to the right of him than to the left. This gives us the feeling that he has room to move into.

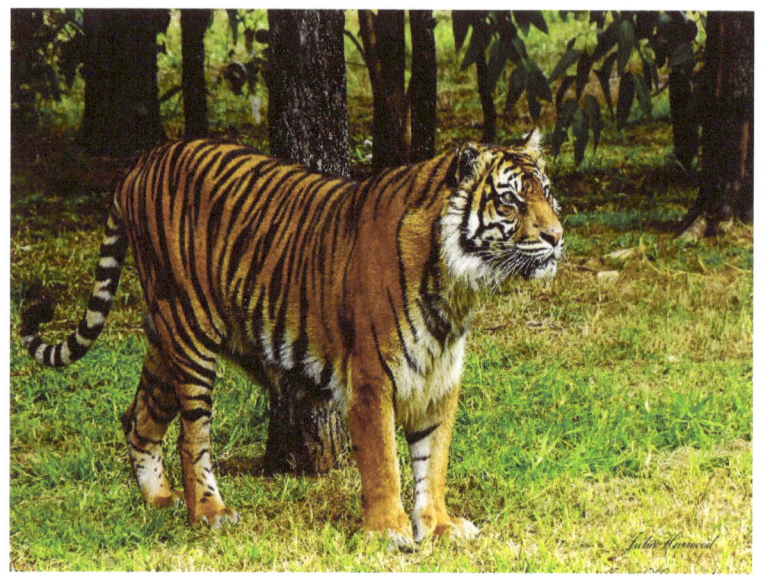

We want to make it look like the animal is engaging with us, so if we are at a zoo where there is a handler feeding them then get to a spot near them where the handler is not in the shot but the animal looks like it is facing towards you.

Whenever you are shooting through enclosures, if possible place your camera right up on the wire so the wire becomes blurred and we don't see it.

The same with glass, but add a polarizing filter to stop any glare or reflections.

Silhouettes make a great animal image so if you are shooting into the light look for times you can use this.

To create a silhouette, expose for sky, have a background free of distractions. Just have the animal, or animal and owner in shot. We need to see the clear shape to identify it, so side on works best and isolated against the sky or an open area would be preferable.

You can get low and highlight them against sky especially if the background is distracting.

Underexpose so that silhouette is full black.

Often an animal will look better when in motion, doing something they love rather than just creating a portrait type image.

Use negative space, this is blank areas in the composition, where there is not much happening, make sure that the negative space is where the animal is facing towards so that the animal looks as if it has room to move.

The first thing we look for in any image with eyes in it is that the eyes are in focus and if possible have a catch-light in them.

This enhances our feeling of interacting with the animal which means we are also engaging with the image.

The next thing we need to look at is the background. Will it enhance the shot and give us a sense of place or is it too busy or does it have unwanted objects in it?

If we want to include the objects in the shot, we can use a wide depth of field and a large f stop or if we just want the focus on the animal and to eliminate the background distractions, then we need a narrow depth of field or a small f stop.

Check there are no objects sticking out of the animal's head, and look for bright objects that might cause distractions.

Our eyes are automatically drawn to bright areas. Move elements or yourself to recompose without the distraction.

To do this, see if by moving a little you can angle out unwanted areas in the background, you can also shoot low but facing up, so that the sky is in the background or shoot from above looking down, so you just have the ground.

While looking at camera angle it is best to get down to the animals level, so you are at the same level as their eyes, but remember, safety first, don't put yourself in harms way.

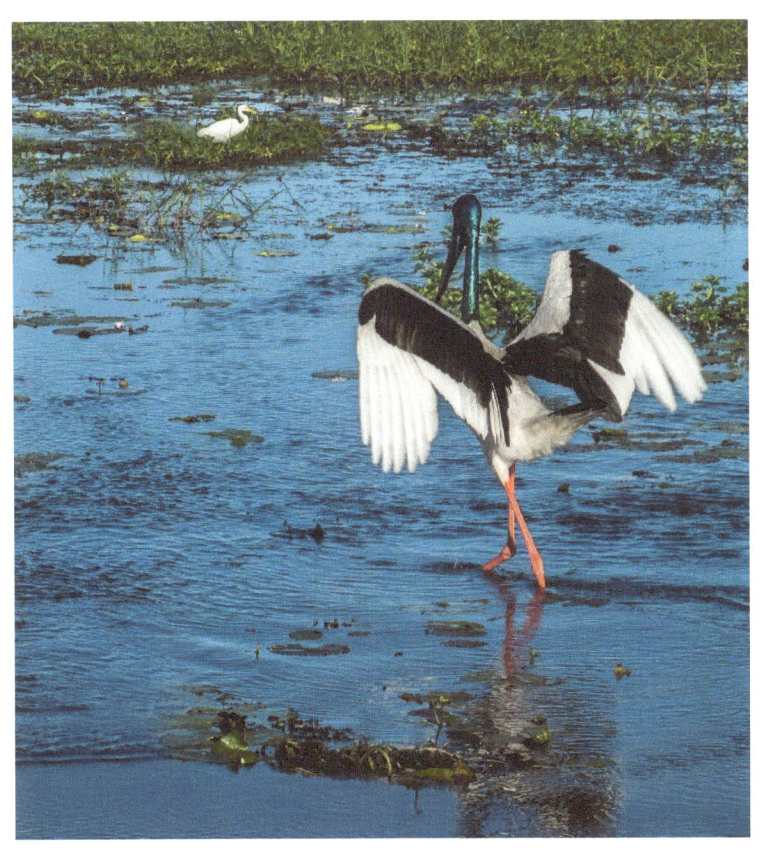

As with human portraits, soft light is best as it gives us soft graduations between shadow and highlighted areas.

Watch harsh shadows in mid day sun, but animals can really pop in sunlight areas so make sure you have sunlight but preferably not the harsh midday sun.

Try to find some shade but still go for catch lights, get animal to look towards sun or light.

Use back lighting or side lighting to create halo around animal
Create these when sun is low in sky.

Use a narrow depth of field to create blurred backgrounds and nice bokeh.

Special note: Watch dogs with black and white as it can be tricky to get both right in the one shot.

For a Canon camera expose to the right, for Nikon cameras expose to the left.

For all other cameras bracket the shot so that you get one shot over exposed, one under-exposed and one correct exposure.

Most cameras have this option under the burst menu.

Canon is better at recovering highlights, Nikon is better at opening up shadows, in post processing so that is why we use these settings.
But test them for your camera.

Showcase the animal's personality, tell a story about the animal.

This can be the best tip for getting great animal shots, they look natural, they captivate us and the pet owners love them.

7. Types of Shots

Types of shots to look for,
Static or still shots can look great if you place dog where you want, get them to sit and take shot.

This makes more of a fine art image and allows you time to set up the composition and check the background for distractions before you set the animal up.

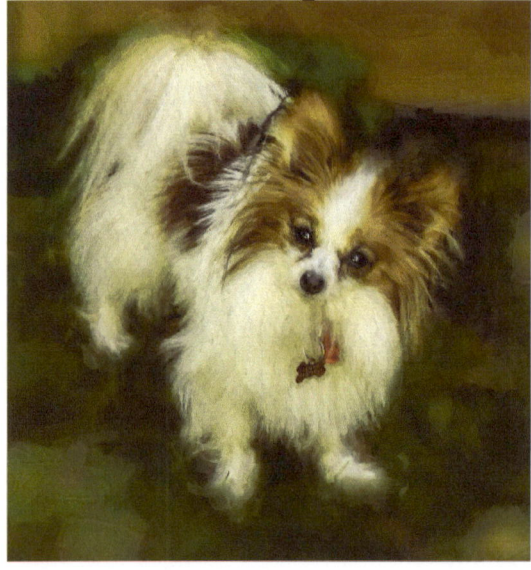

Movement

Contrast static and *motion shots*. Motion shots can be more dynamic and more natural. Again, take time to check the background and lighting before the animal comes into view or starts an activity that will lead to action shots.

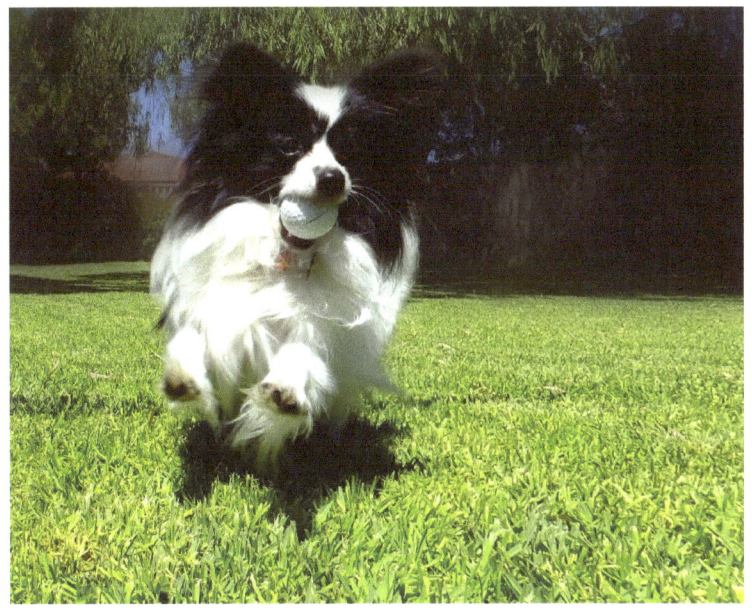

Be sure to get *profile view* as well as a *front on view.*

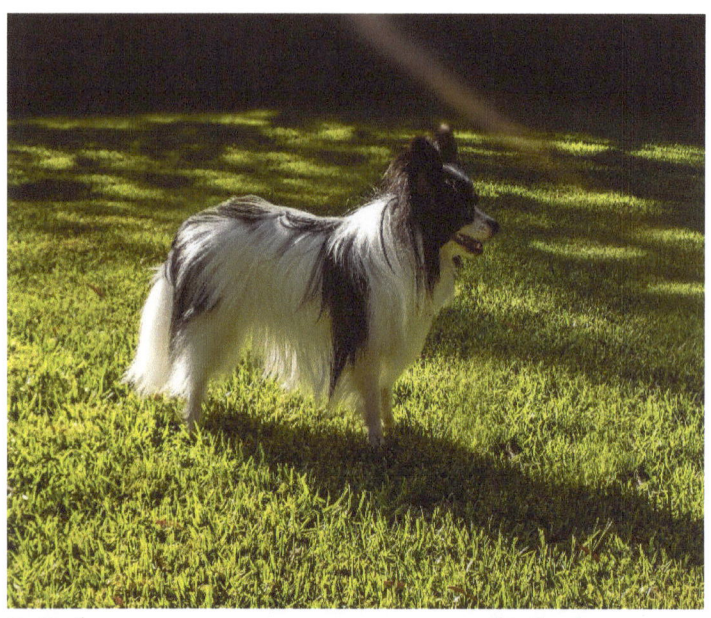

Make sure you get *candid* shots as well as constructed images.

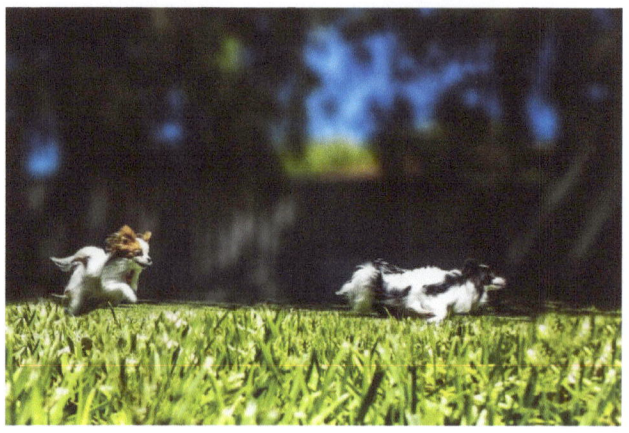

All photos don't have to have the dog looking into the camera.

Experiment with wide angle close up to add some great fun images as it will create comical and distorted images .

Keep *focus on eyes*

Watch your own shadow.

Look around to see what is at the location and what is in the background.

Brown animals look great on a blue background and light colored animals on green or earth toned backgrounds.

Place a treat in what you want the dog to interact with.

Add a scene to help tell a story. You can do this by using a larger depth of field and include their favorite places, toys or people.

Capture *unique things* the animal likes to do.

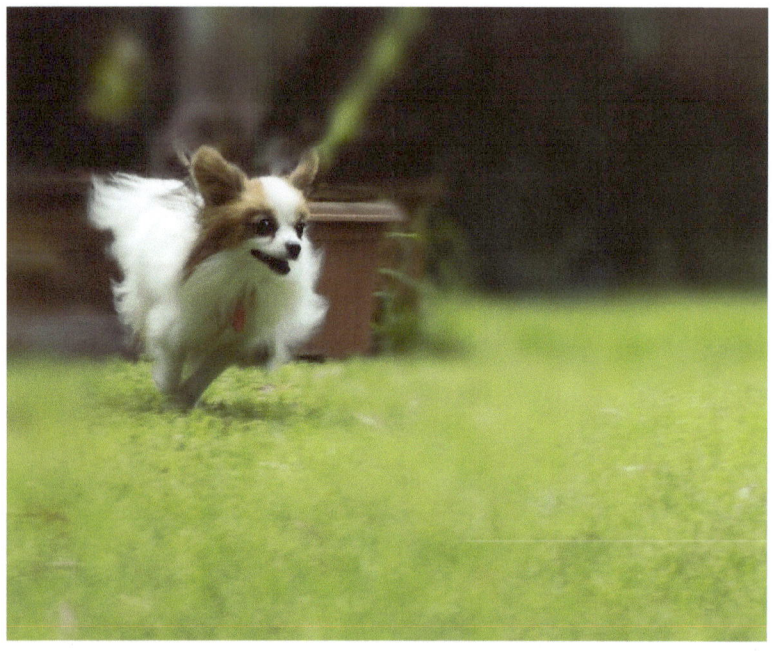

8. Animal Behavior

To successfully capture an animal, it helps to know a little about their behavior and habits, this will help to determine the best time of day to shoot them, it will also let you know if they are becoming stressed.

If an animal is feeling stressed or cornered he may become aggressive, so it's time to move back and give the animal some space.

We don't like strangers poking cameras in our faces, so stay a reasonable distance away and if the animal is scared or appears stressed, walk away.

To capture birds and lots of wild animals it is best to study where they go and then build a hide, this is a camouflaged area for you to sit in and wait for the animal to come into range. Lots of national parks and tourist destinations have these, so ask at the local Rangers office.

8.1. Dog Behavior

<u>Dog Behavior or Language</u>

When the dog's tail is tucked under him/her it usually means they are afraid so this means you need to spend more time with them to get them comfortable with you.

If their ears are laid back against head it means they are uncomfortable with you this is the time to use treats and show dog love to get them to feel comfortable around you.

Avoid eye contact as direct eye contact is a challenge and the dog will not be comfortable with you.

All domestic animals needs love and time to get to trust you, this is why it is important to allow time in your shoot for this getting to know you phase.

Don't force the dog if they are uncomfortable.

A way to make the dog more comfortable with you is to:
Get low to the ground but then turn your back to the dog.

Next place a treat between you and the dog making sure you move slowly.

Then Move treat closer to you and turn side on.

Finally face the dog and see if he/she will take treat from your hand.

You won't get dogs personality if they are uncomfortable or afraid.

If dog is still uncomfortable around you it is time to pull back and use a longer lens.

This will enable the owner to interact and play with the dog and as the dog realizes you are not a treat you may be able to get closer shots later in the shoot.

Be aware when the dog has worked hard at play he/she will be puffing a lot, so allow time for him to recover and make sure that you have water for him or her to drink.

Have someone throw a stick or toy from behind you so that when the dog is coming back he is running towards you.

You can also try panning the camera as the dog is running.

Take lots of images.

Focus on the dog when it is stationary and use af-c when the dog is moving and the focus will follow the dog's movement.

Constantly recompose for the background and look for the best composition.

I will be covering most of the composition rules in my next e-book on Landscapes.

Get action shots, front legs up in air and sand or water flying, be at dog's level and focus on its eyes.

If you haven't or couldn't use fill flash you can add some in post-processing by using these settings.
Exposure 0.35
Contrast 7
Vibrance 1.5

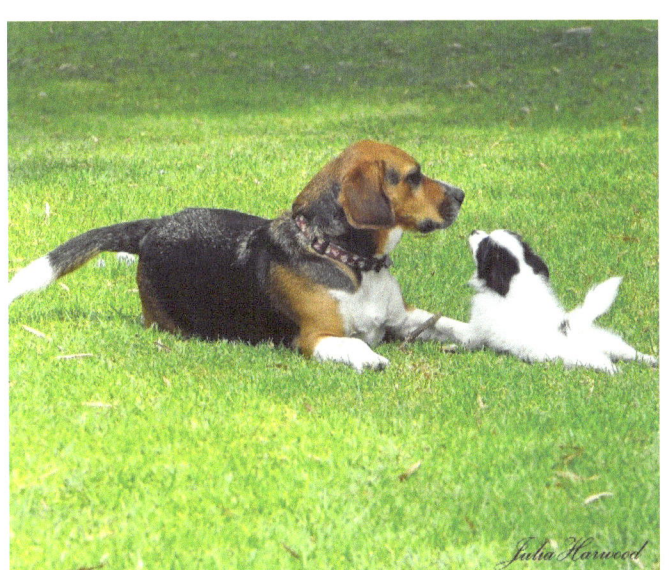

8.2. Cat Behavior

<u>Cats</u>

Rub against you to deposit scent and get your attention.

They meow to communicate with humans, so if you meow back you are communicating with them.

Cats will kneed a surface when they are preparing to lie down and relax.

If a cat's tail is swishing it signals high arousal or impending attack, so if the cat lowers his/her body and is swishing tail they are probably about to pounce, this is the time to direct their energy to a toy and capture the shot.

Cats often have times of what is called "night crazies," which is when they start running around crazily at night, or just "going ballistic." for any other time that they start running around like crazy, jumping off things and are generally out of control.

Ask the owner of the cat if he/she has these at a regular time, they can be great for getting motion shots.

Use treats as in section for dogs.

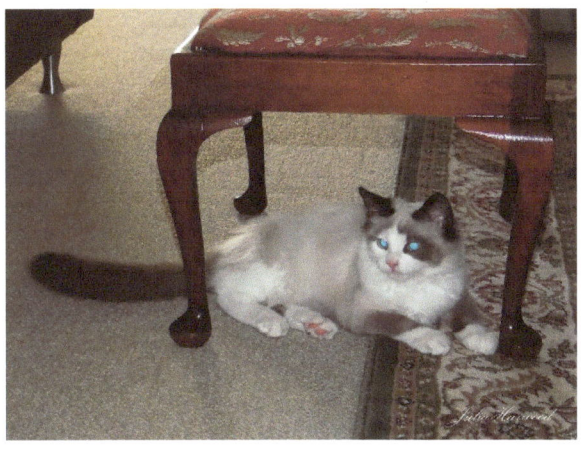

8.3. Horse Behavior

Horses

Let's look at two main groups of animals, prey animals and predators. (Humans fall into the predator category.)

A prey animal is a herbivorous grazing animal and is killed and eaten by predator animals such as a lion or a wolf (humans are considered a predator species, after all we do eat grazing animals).

Horses are part of the equine family that includes Donkeys, Zebra and wild Asses which are also grazing herbivores.
This means they are vegetarian and get their food by grazing.

Amongst the prey species you basically have two behavior types as well. One group stays together when frightened the other group flees.

The best example to distinguish the two types is to look at cattle and sheep as being of the prey species that bunch together for safety, while horses and deer will choose to flee or take flight from danger.

This is very important to know because "flight animals" are much more skittish and will startle more easily than prey animals that bunch together. As a result a flight animal is more easily "traumatized".

Without the ability to flee, flight animals will attack.

Spooking an animal is usually caused by sudden movements or loud noise.

Weather, especially wind can make horses jumpy so be aware of the weather.

Ask the owner to handle the animal and get it to do what you want.

Behaviors to learn.

Watch their ears.
Pricking or facing the ears forward indicates interest. But also watch for flared nostrils, as this means the animal is not comfortable with you yet.

Flattened ears are usually a sign of anger, especially if combined with barring teeth and showing whites of eyes.

If both ears are facing backwards it usually means he is trying to pay attention to a noise behind him.
If his ears flop naturally he is calm and relaxed.

Barred teeth are usually mean that the horse is unhappy, but can also be a sign of nuzzling, look for other signs to indicate if he is scared or just looking for food and attention.

Eyes:
When the horses eyes are half closed, this means the horse is relaxed and calm.

If the tail is between it's legs, it usually means the horse is afraid.

Heavy stamping of feet is usually a sign of fear, light stamping of feet may mean that the horse wants to go for a run.

Bucking is a way of playing and tail will often kink before a horse bucks. Rearing in a foal can be playfulness, but in a stallion it can be a sign of fear.

A relaxed horse's head will normally hang low, but if you can get his attention with something, maybe a carrot, then he will raise his head and often his tail as well.
If they are afraid they will usually run away if they can.

Horses noses:
When wrinkled it usually means disgust or irritation, like when we smell something we don't like.
When the horse stretches his nose out it may mean horse wants grooming, especially if the lower lip is drawn back and the neck extended.

Horse sounds:
Horse sighs are similar to human sighs.

A sigh followed by a shudder is usually the relaxing of muscles and a sign of contentment or relief.

Sighing may also be an expression of boredom.
Nickering is usually a sign of welcome.

Groaning indicates the horse is in pain.

Snorting is often how the horse shows it's excitement.

Neighing needs to be looked at with other body language to know what it means.

It the horse's ears are completely flat and tale swishing, he is in a really bad mood or hungry.

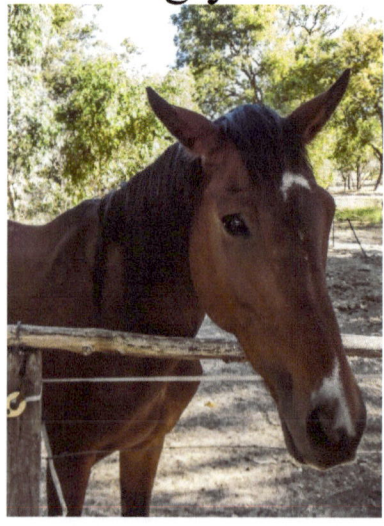

8.4. Zoo Animals, Nocturnal Animals

For the behavior of wild animals contact the local Zoo and speak to the animal's keeper. Also find out when feeding times are .

Also look for open range zoos or see if you can go on a safari as these will give you the most natural images without the animals getting stressed.

When shooting through an enclosure at a zoo, shoot at the widest aperture available on your lens, while getting as close as possible to the obstruction or enclosure.

This is good for wire enclosures.
F5.6 or wider shutter speed at least
1/500 if moving animal, 1/250 if
resting.

Use servo or continuous focus and
burst mode.

Nocturnal animals
A note here: please just keep in
mind the ethics of nature
photography in mind ... flash
photography can be detrimental
http://www.wildlife-pictures-
online....ght-drive.html

Night photography of animals
usually requires special gear.

A number of photographers offer
specific night time tours to
photograph animals at night.

Generally they use an infrared or capacitative trigger to set off an infrared flash when the animal passes within a certain range.

To capture a nocturnal animal, set up in an area you know the animal you want to photograph will walk near. For example, along a known game trail or near a waterhole.

Have an external flash or two mounted to the side along the trail, make sure you have a red gel or a red cellophane cover on them so as not to affect the animal's eyes and then fire them from the camera when the animal comes into position.

You would have to be in a blind or up in a tree most likely with a remote set-up for your flashes.

You can put out a salt lick for some of the larger animals or find out what their usual prey is and use that.

Go to your preselected vantage point when the moon is out so you have some background light.

Take a flash-light to help you see the buttons on the camera and, if need be, to spotlight the animal you are trying to photograph.

Use a red light source, since it is less visible to animals. If you don't have a red bulb, you can cover the flash-light with red cellophane paper.

You can read more here:http://www.ehow.com/how_58 95303_pictures-wildlife-night.html

It is best to shoot when there is a full moon as this will give you the most light and enable a faster shutter speed.

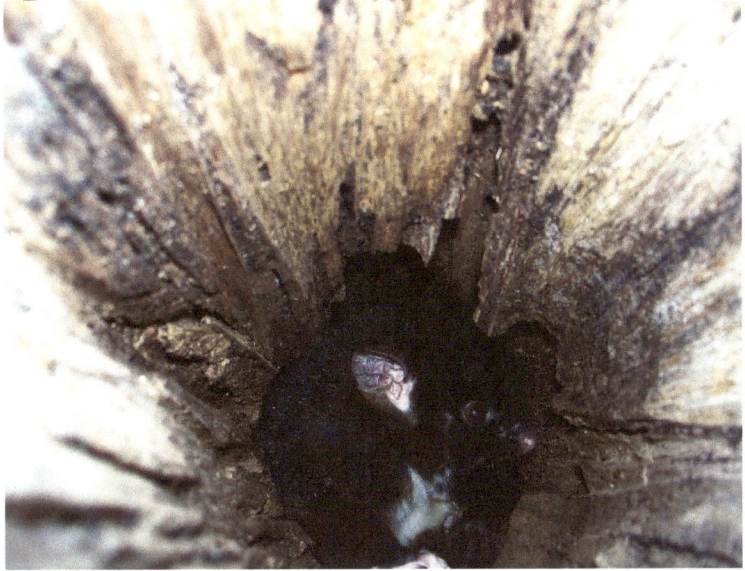

Ducks or water-birds
Lie down on the bank of the river to get at eye level, blur background, look for nice colors or reflections in water.

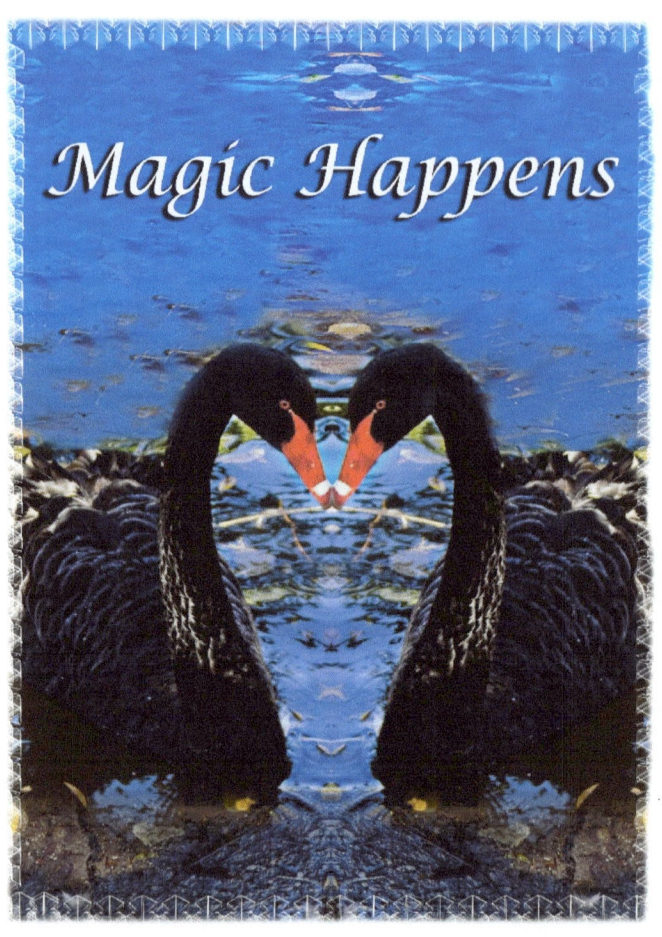

Magic Happens

Capturing life is more engaging than shots of sleeping animals.

So try to capture expression, detail and personality.

Animals are often more active between 4 and 5pm. Again get at their eye level if possible.

Zoo
Zoos often have wire or glass enclosures that the animals are kept in.

The best way to not have these in your shot is to shoot at the widest aperture available on your lens, while getting as close as possible to the obstruction. If it is a glass enclosure use a polarizing filter as well to minimise reflections.
F5.6 or wider shutter speed at least 1/500 if moving animal, 1/250 if resting.

Use servo or continuous focus and burst mode .

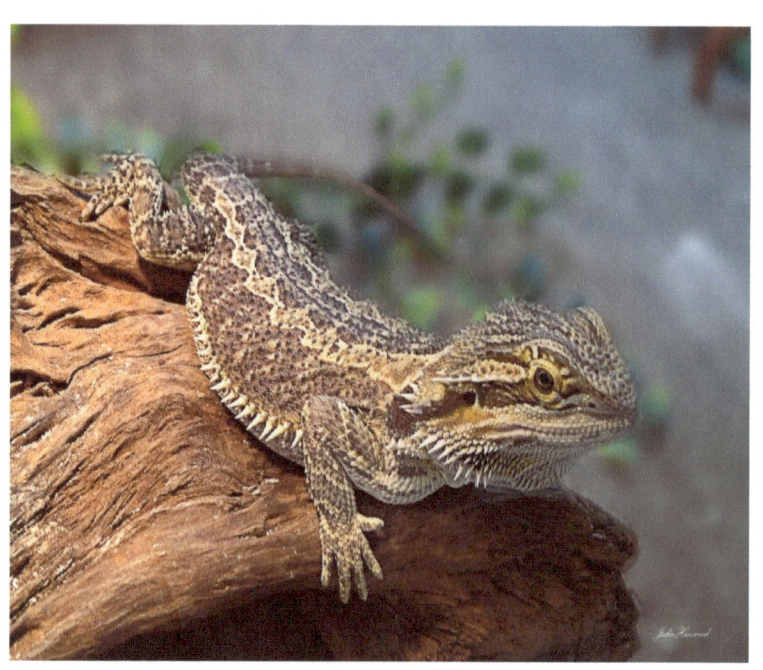

8.5. Insects

I also want to mention insects here as there are a few people who refrigerate the insects before they shoot them so that they are still.

We are interested in shooting nature so let's try to capture them in their natural environment.

Sometimes we need to photograph animals for scientific journals or research so I will include the information you need to refrigerate them, but again, try to stay with nature as much as possible.

In the early morning insects are slower and therefore easier to photograph and they will often sparkle with dew.

Use f8-f11, Put a colored card behind the insect if the background is busy.

If you need to photograph them for scientific purposes then the following may help.

Close ups - capture insect, place in refrigerator, then shoot.
Times for refrigeration:
Large insects: 5 minutes (dragonflies, bumblebees, butterflies)
Medium insects: 3 minutes (shield bugs, ladybugs, large spiders)
Delicate insects: 1 minute (damselflies, crane flies)
Each time interval, open the fridge and check on the bug.
If they are still walking around, they aren't close.

If they are pretty still, but clinging to the side of the dish, they are close.

If they are very still and aren't clinging to anything, they are just right (as long as they aren't dead).

The first few times you may lose your bug, but other times you will swear that you killed it, only to have it revive when it warms up and go on like nothing happened.

The other way is to put the insect in a plastic container with some dry ice. The CO_2 will sublimate both cooling and putting the bug to sleep.

When the bug quits moving, remove the bug and take your shot. In a few moments the bug will wake up and fly (or move) away.

This is an old trick that magicians have used to reanimate a dead insect.

Read more at:http://www.pentaxforums.com/forums/38-photographic-technique/196481-refrigeration-insects-macro-photography.html#ixzz3TZcmlEEd

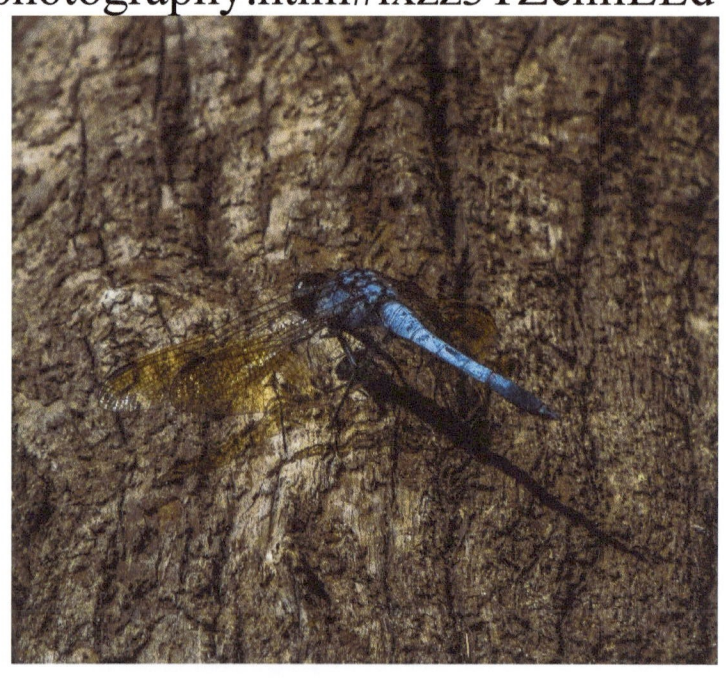

9. Cheat Sheets

Before the shoot
Questions to ask
What toys do they like?
What tricks does he or she do?
Are there any parks or areas that he/she visits regularly?
How do they behave off leash?
How does your animal react to strangers and other dogs/animals?
Do they know any commands?
Do they have any quirky things or tricks they do?
What are their favorite toys?
Are they food motivated or attention motivated?
How do you get their attention?
Where do they spend most of their time?

During the shoot
Start with something they are comfortable
doing.
Be patient with animal.
Get down at animals level.
Get animals attention and looking at camera.
Even treats lose value over time. Start off
with just normal animal biscuits.
Use a favorite treat for getting their attention.
Dogs and cats can be trained by having a
small clicker or squeaker and click or squeak,
then give treat, they quickly make the
association and then click it when you are
ready to take shot and they will look at you in
expectation.
Give lots of praise as well as treats
If something is distracting the animal, place
yourself between animal and distraction

Gear to take
Camera

Flash with movable head to bounce

Soft box, you can put any light in these

A lens with as low stop as possible, preferably F1.4 to f2.8 that has Quick focus and image stabilzation

Focal length 85mm full body shot head shot 35mm more wide angle to show setting, also use for looking down from above at dog.

70-200mm f2.8 action lens

Use fastest card you can afford

Carry a spare battery and spare cards.

Reflector

A Lens hood, as it protects the lens and keeps dog nose off lens.

If shooting wild animals then a tripod to stabilize the long zoom will help. Remember to turn Image stabilisation (IS) off.

Settings
Al servo mode af-c focus mode keep shutter half pressed so camera can keep focusing

Use burst mode

Use sports mode, Shutter Priority or manual settings with shutter speed 1/500 or higher.

Avoid mixing indoor and outdoor light.

Exposure
If going from light to shade use AP or A priority

If this isn't an issue, use S shutter priority to freeze action

Pay attention to the background, look for any distractions and move them, angle them out or use a narrow aperture, low f number to blur them out.

Watch your own shadow

Look around to see what is at the location and what is in the background.

Brown animals look great on blue, light colored animals on green or earth tones.

Dog behavior

Tucked tail usually means they are afraid (spend time to get them used to you)

Ears laid back against head means they are uncomfortable with you (use treats and show dog love to get them comfortable)

Avoiding direct eye contact as this a challenge and the dog will not be comfortable with you. (needs love and time to trust you)

Cat behavior

Rub against you to deposit scent and get your attention

They meow to communicate with humans, so meow back.

Cats kneed a surface when they are preparing to lie down and relax.

If a cat's tail is swishing it signals high arousal or impending attack.

If cat lowers body and is swishing tail they are probably about to pounce, direct their energy to a toy and capture the shot.

Look for times cat is most active.

Horse Behavior

Ears:
Pricking or forward indicates interest.

Flattened ears are usually a sign of anger, watch for barred teeth and showing whites of eyes.

Barred teeth are usually unhappy but can be a sign of nuzzling.

If both ears facing back it usually means he is trying to pay attention to a noise behind him.

If his ears flop naturally he is calm and relaxed.

Eyes:
Eyes half closed, horse is relaxed and calm.

Tail between legs is normally a sign of fear.

Heavy stamping sign of fear, light stamping horse may want to go for a run.

Bucking is a way of playing.
Tail will often kink before a horse bucks.
Rearing in a foal can be playfulness.

In a stallion it can be a sign of fear.

A relaxed horses head will normally hang low.

Get attention with something, maybe a carrot, then he will raise his head and often his tail as well.

If they are afraid they will usually run away if they can.

Horses noses:
When wrinkled it usually means disgust or irritation.

Long nose may mean horse wants grooming, the lower lip is drawn back and the neck extended.

Watch for flared nostrils as that means he is not comfortable with you yet.

House sounds:
Horse sighs are similar to human sighs.

Sigh followed by a shudder is usually relaxing muscles and contentment or relief.

Can be an expression of boredom.

Nickering is usually a sign of welcome.

Groaning indicates pain. Snorting is often the horse showing it is excited.

Neighing needs to be looked at with other body language to know what it means.

Horse's ears completely flat and tale swishing, he is in a really bad mood or hungry.

Insects
Insects look for in the early morning
Remember for all animals, red flash is best!!!

Types of shots to look for

Static shots (still), place animal where you want, get them to sit and take shot.
Motion shots can be more dynamic and more natural.

Be sure to get profile as well as front on.

Make sure you get candid shots as well as constructed images.

All photos don't have to have dog looking into the camera.

Experiment with wide angle close up to add some great fun images.

Keep focus on eyes.

Stick a treat in what you want the dog to interact with.

Add a scene to help tell a story.
Capture unique things the animal likes to do.